THE MODERN BASSIST ™

Supplementary Book 1

LEARNING THE BLUES

By JOSEPH LILORE

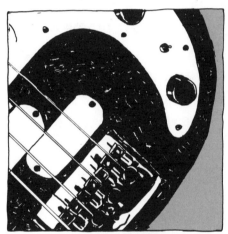

Art Direction: Michael Connelly
Cover Illustration: Gayle Erikson

Managing Editor: David Jessie
Editorial Director: Tony Esposito

CONTENTS

EVOLUTION OF "THE BLUES"

After the Civil War, many freed slaves migrated to New Orleans and the Mississippi Delta region, especially Will Dockery's farm, near Clarksdale Mississippi, where the "Blues" evolved. A direct line can be drawn from the Delta to Chicago, where this music grew into a more sophisticated sound. The Illinois Central Railroad carried many great Bluesmen, like McKinly Morgonfield (Muddy Waters), from the Delta to the north, where they developed their individual styles.

Others moved to Memphis, and eventually into Sam Phillips' small recording studio, where Rhythm and Blues changed into Rock and Roll in the early 50's.
The sound of the Delta became the cornerstone of today's modern music.

The early Blues was characterized by melodies, based on the Blues Scale, sung or played against a standard twelve bar chord progression. It was usually divided into three sections, four bars each. The melody of each section didn't last the complete four measures, which left a hole or gap. This gap was filled in with improvised bits of melody called "riffs", which became an integral part of this music. Gradually the musicians began extending these riffs throughout the whole 12 bars. This transition from "set melodies" to improvised riffs is the basis of Jazz and Rock.

With this book you will learn how to use the tools needed to create Blues solos.

FINGERBOARD DIAGRAM

The Bass Fingerboard will be illustrated in the following manner. It will be divided into sections by raised metal ridges called "FRETS".

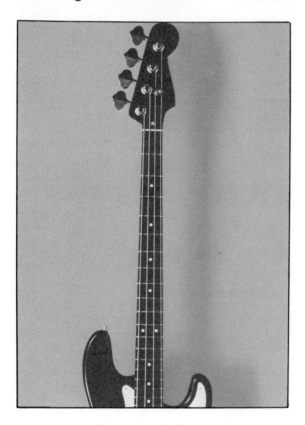

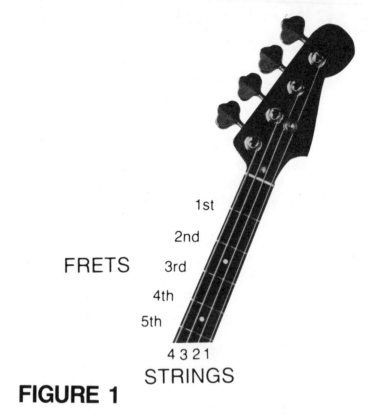

FRETS — 1st, 2nd, 3rd, 4th, 5th

4 3 2 1
STRINGS

FIGURE 1

FINGER PLACEMENT

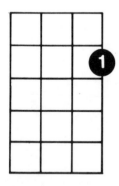

Finger Placement on Fingerboard

FIGURE 2

The circular notation in the diagram instructs you to press down the 1st string on the 2nd fret with your 1st finger.

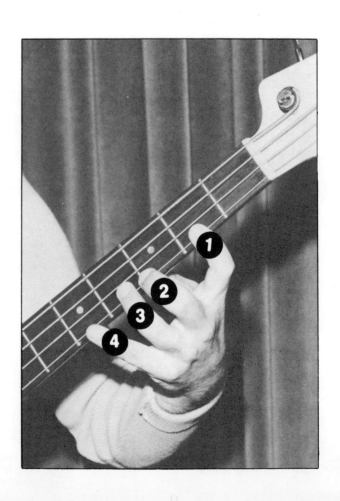

TABLATURE

By this method, even if you can't read music, you'll be able to play all the examples and exercises with the accompanying record.

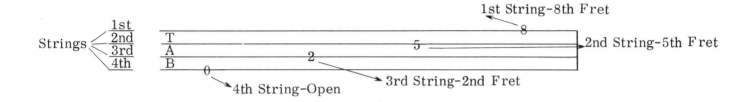

FIGURE 3

TUNING

● Tune your bass to the tuning section on the accompanying record.

THE BLUES PROGRESSION

The standard Blues progression is twelve (12) bars long. It is composed of the I7(Tonic)-IV7 (Sub-dominant)-V7 (Dominant 7th) chords of any given key.* There are many variations of this basic form which are introduced in this book, but this is the foundation and standard.

At this point listen carefully to the individual sound of each chord and their progression from one to another.

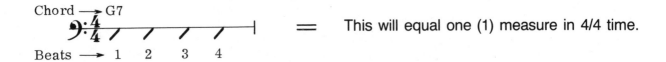   =   This will equal one (1) measure in 4/4 time.

● *RECORDED EXAMPLE #1*

All chord progressions will be shown in the following manner:

"G" BLUES PROGRESSION

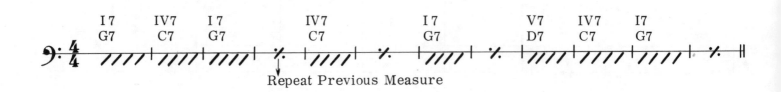

*The Blues is the only style of music that stresses the Dominant 7th on the I and IV chords along with the V. The tension of the Dominant 7th chord is one of the most significant aspects of the Blues. For more information on chord and key construction see Warner Bros. "The Modern Bassist - A Complete Method" by Joseph Lilore.

7

SCALE FORMS

All the Blues scales introduced in this book are illustrated on fingerboard diagrams with finger patterns called "scale forms".

"G" Blues Scale Form

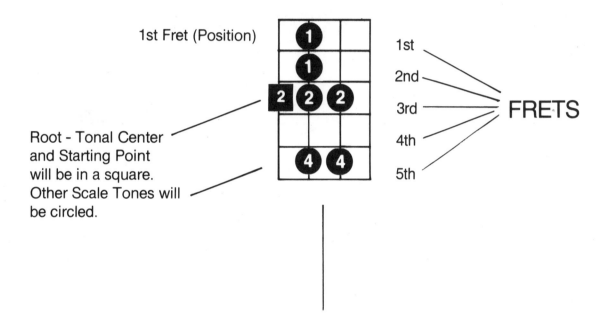

TABLATURE- Blues Scale Form

THE BLUES SCALE - BASIC

The notes of a Blues melody are based on the Blues scale. This scale is composed of the 1st- Minor 3rd*- 3rd- 4th- 5th- Minor 7th notes of the Parallel Major Scale.**

● *RECORDED EXAMPLE #2*

G MAJOR SCALE   G MAJOR SCALE FORM

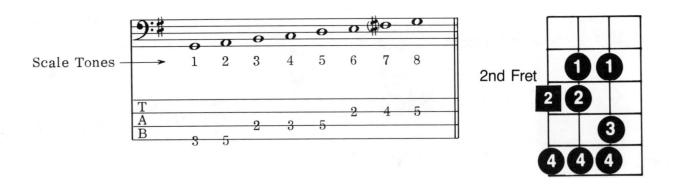

Compare

G BLUES SCALE - BASIC   G BLUES SCALE FORM - BASIC

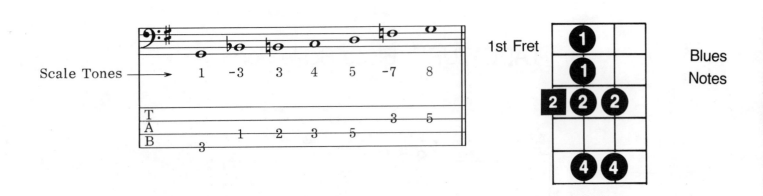

Minor: 3rd and 7th tones are lowered one-half step. The minor 3rd and minor 7th are called the "Blues Notes". These are the notes which approximate the original Blues singers' ability to bend certain tones with their voices, creating the unique "Blues Effect".

**Scale Construction- Page 46

OUTLINE - EARLY BLUES

The "Early Blues", always sung, related stories of sadness from an occurence, such as a lost love or daily hardships. These were three lines of text: The first two were identical (the statement), and the third was contrasting (the answer).

EX: 1.   My baby's gone and left me

    2.   My baby's gone and left me

    3.   What am I gonna do?

The music reflects the text with three 4-bar sections. The actual musical phrases* are only two bars long, leaving a 2-bar break at the end of each line. This break was "filled in" with improvised** bits of melody supplied by one of the accompanying instruments. This procedure was referred to as the "call" and "response".

The three primary chords- I- IV- V- accompanied the melody in the following patterns:

(● *Recorded Ex. #1 Page 6)*

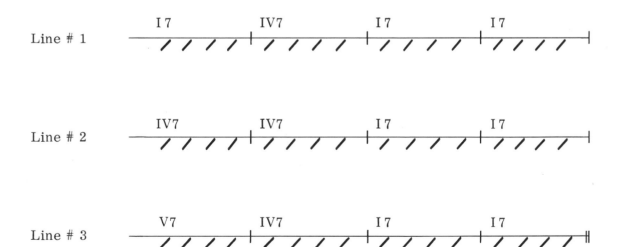

* See Musical Phrase - Page 14.
** Improvised - created spontaneously as it is played - "ad libbed". Also known as "break", "hole", or "jazz strain".

● *RECORDED EXAMPLE #3 - EARLY BLUES WITH RIFFS*

In this example, the melody (call) and response (riff) are based on the G Blues Scales. The melody is played on the guitar, and the response on the bass, so you can hear the separation of both parts clearly. Both parts are written in the Bass Clef with tablature so you can play along with the record.

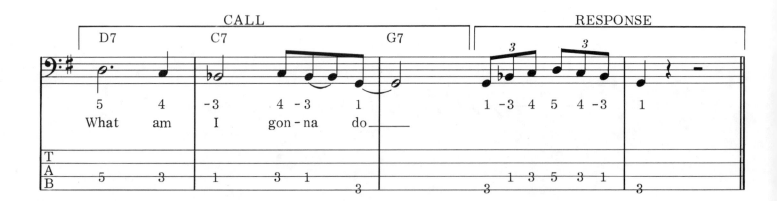

One of the most important things you can do is listen to all the great Blues artists. To play "The Blues" you must listen to "The Blues". Following are some of the greatest Blues artists of all time:

B.B. King	Michael Bloomfield	Charley Patton	Eric Clapton
Kenny Burrell	Son House	Albert King	Jimi Hendrix
Robert Johnson	Willie Brown	"Sonny Boy" Williamson	Blind Lemon Jefferson
Howlin' Wolf	Robert Nighthawk	Johnny Shines	Jimmy Rogers
Robert Lockwood	John Lee Hooker	Ike Turner	and countless others

● *RECORDED EXAMPLE #4 - EARLY BLUES WITH FREER RESPONSE*

At first the riffs were simple responses to the melody, but gradually they developed into a freer style. Play along with the following example, which illustrates this point.

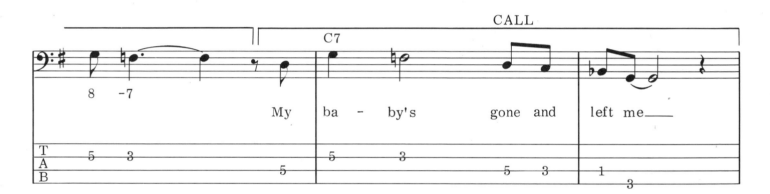

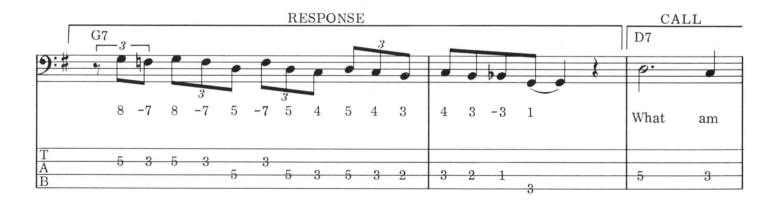

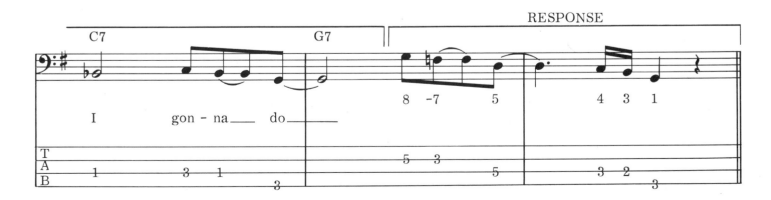

● *RECORDED EXAMPLE #5 - SOLO STYLE*

As the musicians experimented creating musically interesting riffs, they gradually began to extend these riffs into complete solos lasting one or more choruses (Blues Chorus = 12 bars). These solos were created spontaneously (ad libbed). Musicians were judged on how original, creative, technically proficient and musical they could be. This became the foundation of "blues" improvising and its off-shoots, Jazz and Rock. In this example, the melody is in the style of the extended, improvised riffs. It consists of:

(1) Improvised melody (solo) based on the "G" blues scale and

(2) 12 bar blues progression on "G".

Play along with the record, listening carefully to the effect of the Blues scale against the progression:

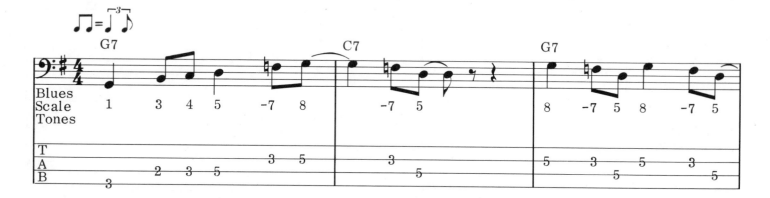

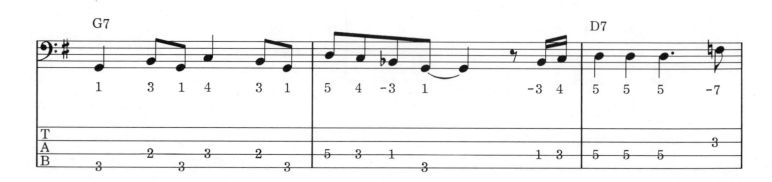

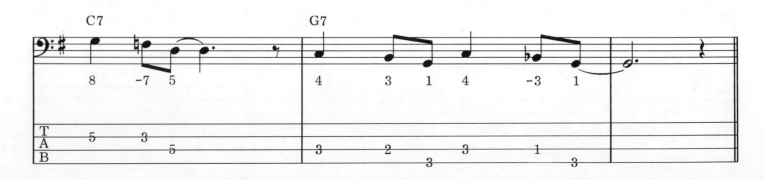

BASIC GUIDELINES TO IMPROVISING YOUR OWN SOLOS

Now you will begin improvising your own solos. We'll start with some basic guidelines to help you. As you get better you can change these guidelines to suit your own style. For now, it's to your advantage to follow them closely.

The best approach is the same as a child learning how to talk. We'll start off with short phrases and bits of musical "speech" and then enlarge them into complete thoughts until you're telling a musical story.

At first we will "talk" without accompaniment and then we'll combine our improvised melodies (solos) with the Blues 12-bar chord progression:

(1) Use the notes of the "G" Blues Scale.
(2) Stress the Blues notes.

MEMORIZE

G BLUES SCALE - ONE OCTAVE

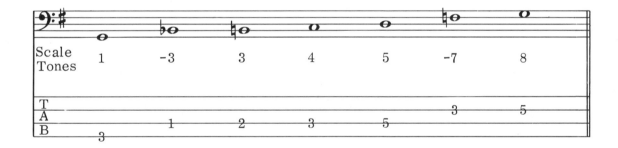

(3) Start off very simply, paying careful attention to the sound created when certain notes are played. These sounds should be thought of as colors and you are the artist.

● *RECORDED EXAMPLE #6*

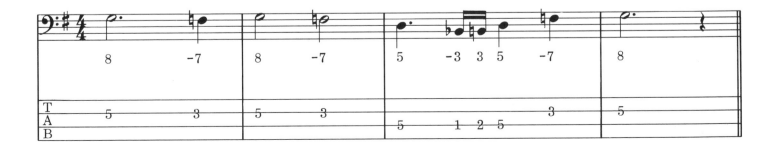

(4) Change rhythms (speed of notes) and direction for variety.

● *RECORDED EXAMPLE #7*

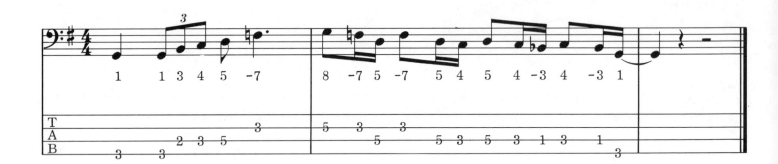

(5) Change the phrasing. A musical phrase is like a clause or sentence in a paragraph. When writing, you combine related sentences, clauses and phrases to convey a thought or tell a story. In music it's exactly the same - you must convey to the listener a logical and complete musical statement through the combination of these phrases. Two-bar phrases are the most commonly used in the Blues.

MUSICAL PHRASE

The following examples will be musical phrases, two measures long, based on the Blues scale. When improvising your own phrases, try to say something to the listener that makes sense. Your choice of notes, movement and direction will determine your success. Study the examples carefully as a guide to various possibilities. Play along with each example, capturing its feel and style.

● *RECORDED EXAMPLE #8*

EX. A) This example ends on the main note (root) of the Blues scale used, ending the phrase in the same manner as a period ends a sentence.

● *RECORDED EXAMPLE #9*

EX. B) This example ends on a scale tone rather than the root, giving the impression of a pause - similar to a comma in a sentence.

● *RECORDED EXAMPLE #10*

EX. C) You can begin a phrase on the root or any other scale tone you wish.

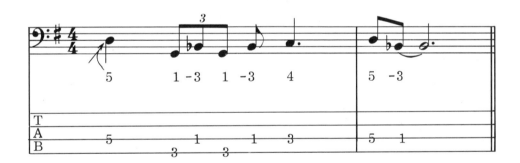

Practice creating your own two-bar phrases based on the notes of the basic Blues scale. Imagine you're talking to someone in short sentences. Start and end each phrase with different scale tones.

FOUR MEASURE PHRASES

The following examples are all four measures in length. You can use two short phrases (EX. A), or one long phrase (EX. B).

● *RECORDED EXAMPLE #11*

Example A

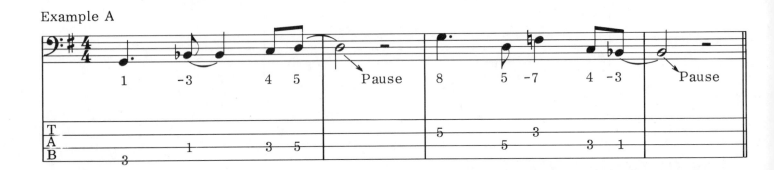

In Example "A", notice that the first phrase does not end on the root. Keep this in mind when combining and relating two short phrases. This is done so the listener will not feel it's the end of the thought, but only a pause. However, the end of the fourth measure can end either on the root or just another scale tone.

● *RECORDED EXAMPLE #12*

Example B

In Example "B", there is no pause halfway through - it is one continuous phrase leading to a definite end or a pause, depending on choice of note.

Practice making as many four-bar phrases as possible, using the techniques covered - two short or one long phrase, starting and stopping on various scale tones.
You are now ready to improvise phrases of varying lengths against the Blues progression and create your own Blues solos.

IMPROVISED SOLOS

These solos will be constructed of two-bar and four-bar phrases, joined together in the same way sentences combine to form paragraphs. Keep playing Progression #13 over and over, constantly improvising new solos.

● *RECORDED EXAMPLE #13*

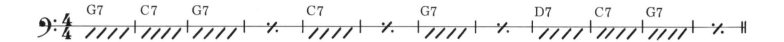

UNEVEN PHRASES

At this point you should experiment creating phrases of uneven duration. At first, they may seem strange, but with practice you'll definitely add variation to your solos.

● *RECORDED EXAMPLE #14*

EX. #1 One Measure (Fragment)

EX. #2 Three Measures

THE FLATTED 5th (Diminished 5th)

The Diminished 5th* (Augmented 4th) is often added to the basic scale for tonal variety.

Example on "G"- Memorize

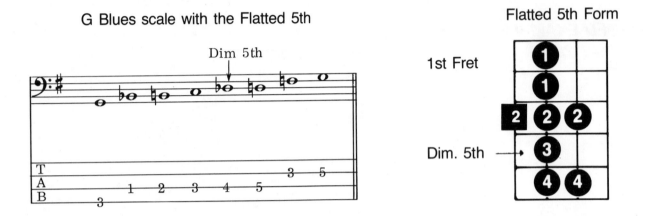

G Blues scale with the Flatted 5th

Flatted 5th Form

● **RECORDED EXAMPLE #15**

This example stresses the use of the Flatted 5th in the melody. Play along with the melody, analyzing the sound created with the use of this new tone (color).

*See Intervals; page 47

Now that you've played the ''G'' Blues scale with the flatted 5th, you should play Recorded Example #13 improvising your own melodies (lines), emphasizing this new tone.

THE ADDED-NOTE BLUES SCALE

When improvising, you may also use the 2nd and 6th notes of the Major scale. This will soften the effect of the basic scale. Stressing the basic, basic with Flatted 5th or Added-Note Blues scale, will add variety to your solos.

Example on ''G''-Memorize

''G'' Added-Note Blues Scale

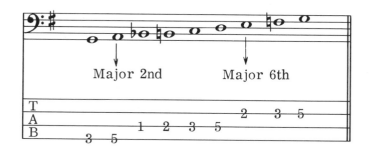

Added-Note Blues Scale Form

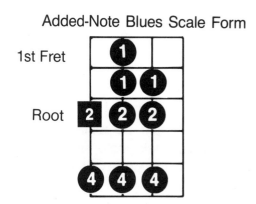

● *RECORDED EXAMPLE #16*

This example stresses the use of the added-note Blues scale. The added-notes are marked. Play along with this example, listening carefully to the added notes.

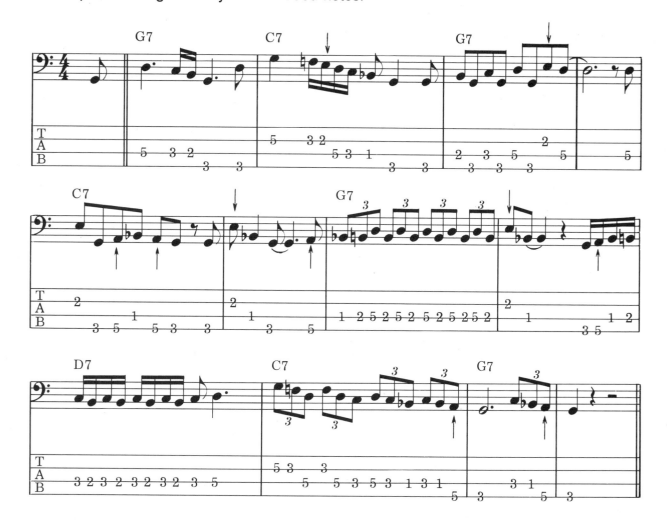

Improvise your own solos to Recorded Example #13 using the added-note Blues scale.

COMBINED BLUES SCALES

● *RECORDED EXAMPLE #17*

Up to this point you've studied three Blues scales on "G":

1. Basic

2. Basic with Flatted 5th

3. Added-note.

The following example combines all three types. Play along with the record as with the previous examples. This example features a slightly altered chord progression, which is typical in the Jazz Blues idiom. It is basically the same as the original progression, but various chords are substituted in the progression, adding to the complexity and tonal color.

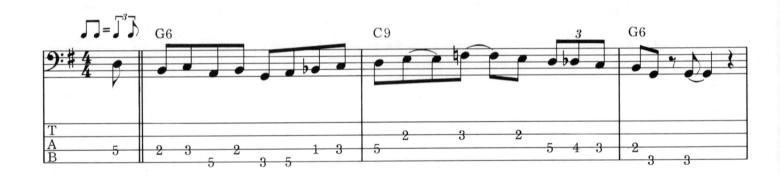

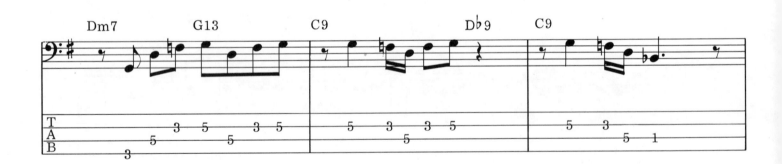

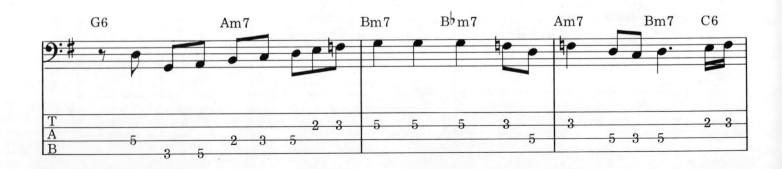

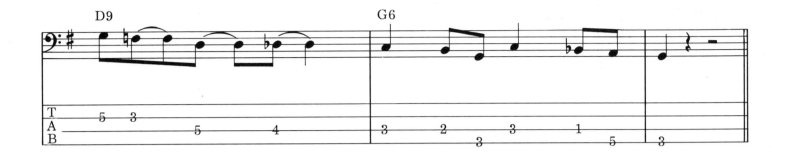

● RECORDED EXAMPLE #18

Improvise your own Blues solos to Recorded Example #18 using:

1. G Basic Scale

2. G Basic Scale with Flatted 5th

3. G Added-note Scale

4. All three combined. Experiment alternating and combining the three types.
Example #18 will have the same chords as Example #17, but the example solo has been taken out.

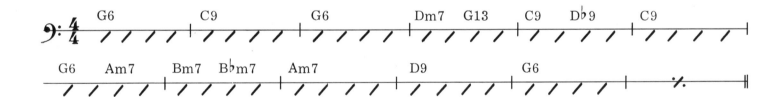

For more on Chords and Extensions see Warner Bros. ''The Modern Bassist- A Complete Method'' by Joseph Lilore - Page 79.

MINOR BLUES

Another variation of the twelve (12) bar progression is the Minor Blues. It is generally composed of the Im-IVm- V7 and VI major 7 or VI7. Use the Natural Minor Scale* when you improvise against this progression. It is composed of the 1st- 2nd- Minor 3rd- 4th- 5th- Minor 6th- Minor 7th notes of the parallel Major scale. The Flatted 5th can be added.

MEMORIZE - "G" NATURAL MINOR

NATURAL MINOR FORM - FLATTED 5th ADDED

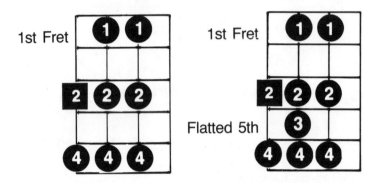

● *RECORDED EXAMPLE #19*

Play along with the following example:

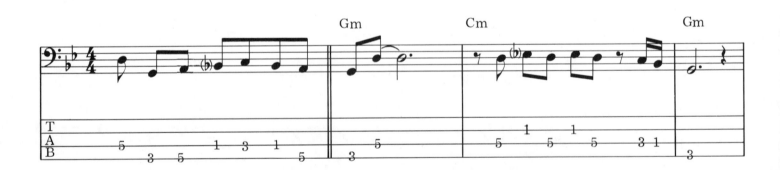

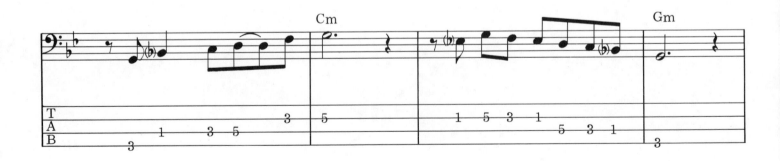

*See Minor Scales- Page 48

● **RECORDED EXAMPLE #20**

This is the same as Example #19, but the example solo has been taken out. Improvise your own solos using:

1. The G Natural Minor Scale

2. The G Natural Minor Scale with the Flatted 5th

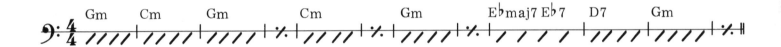

Now that you have studied the most common methods of improvising in the Blues style, the rest of the keys and related scales will be added.

The Major 5th is stressed against the VI major 7th. The Flatted 5th is stressed against the VI7.

BLUES SCALES - MOVABLE FORMS

All Blues scales will be learned through "movable" finger patterns (forms). As before, the notes of each scale will be shown on the fingerboard diagram with a hollow circle. The root (tonal center and starting point) will be in a square.

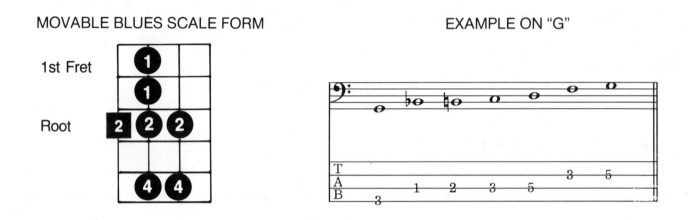

MOVABLE BLUES SCALE FORM   EXAMPLE ON "G"

The above form, which was learned on the "G", is movable. As you play it in a different position, a new scale is created. The position is determined by whatever fret your finger is over, not necessarily by the root.

EXAMPLE:

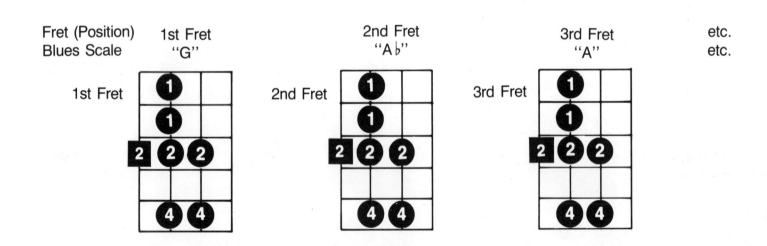

| Fret (Position) | 1st Fret | 2nd Fret | 3rd Fret | etc. |
| Blues Scale | "G" | "A♭" | "A" | etc. |

BLUES SCALE - GROUP IV (4)

Group IV Blues scales have their root on the fourth (4th) string.

GROUP IV BLUES SCALE FORM

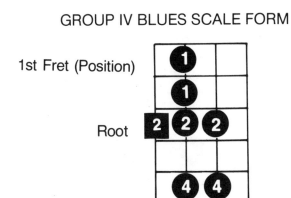

EXAMPLE ON "G"

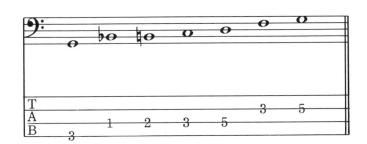

This form played in the following positions will create these Blues scales.

Fret (Position)	1st	2nd	3rd	4th	5th	6th	7th	8th	9th	10th	11th	12th
Major Scale	G	Ab	A	Bb	B	C	C♯	D	Eb	E	F	F♯
Enharmonic Name					Cb		Db					Gb

Practice this Blues scale form chromatically (half-steps) up and down the fingerboard - one scale per measure.

● *RECORDED EXAMPLE #21*

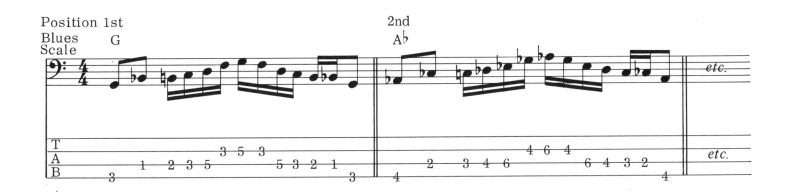

Now that you've mastered the basic scale form, we will add in the three variations we have studied. They are related, and, therefore, "movable" in the same manner.

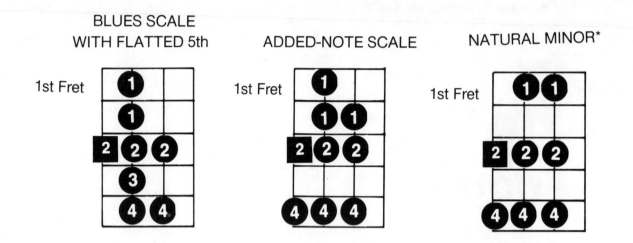

BLUES SCALE WITH FLATTED 5th   ADDED-NOTE SCALE   NATURAL MINOR*

1st Fret

BLUES - ALL KEYS

The various kinds of Blues progressions in all the possible keys are now listed. Improvise to each recorded progression using the appropriate scale, which is also given. Experiment with the basic scale and its variations.

● **RECORDED EXAMPLE #22**

BLUES IN "C" MAJOR

Use "C" Blues scale and variations - 6th position

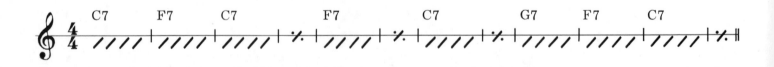

● **RECORDED EXAMPLE #23**

BLUES IN "F" MAJOR

Use "F" Blues scale and variations - 11th position

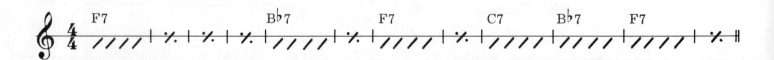

*Used in Minor blues. Remember, Flatted 5th can be added.

● *RECORDED EXAMPLE #24*

BLUES IN "B♭" MAJOR

Use "B♭" Blues scale and variations - 4th position

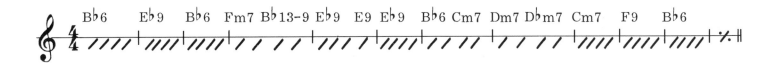

● *RECORDED EXAMPLE #25*

BLUES IN "E♭" MINOR

Use "E♭" natural minor scale - 9th position

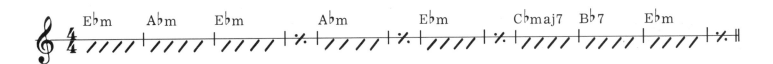

● *RECORDED EXAMPLE #26*

BLUES IN "A♭" MAJOR

Use "A♭" Blues scale and variations - 2nd position

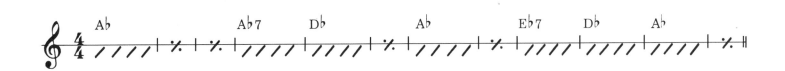

● *RECORDED EXAMPLE #27*

BLUES IN "D♭" MAJOR

Use "D♭" Blues scale and variations - 7th position

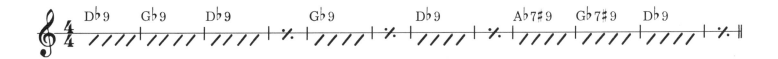

● *RECORDED EXAMPLE #28*

BLUES IN "G♭" MAJOR

Use "G♭" Blues scale and variations - 12th position

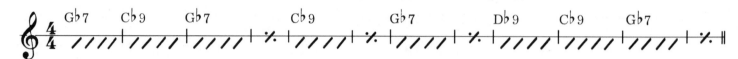

● *RECORDED EXAMPLE #29*

BLUES IN "B" MINOR

Use "B" natural minor scale - 5th position

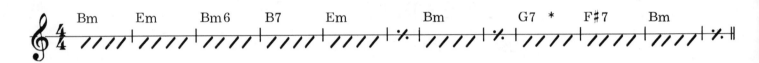

● *RECORDED EXAMPLE #30*

BLUES IN "E" MAJOR

Use "E" Blues scale and variations

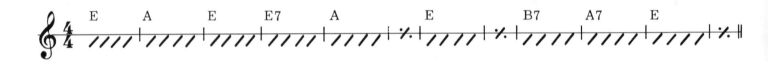

● *RECORDED EXAMPLE #31*

BLUES IN "A" MAJOR

Use "A" Blues scale and variations - 3rd position

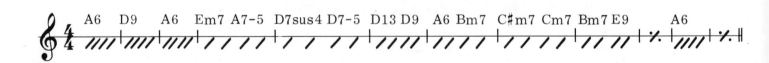

● *RECORDED EXAMPLE #32*

BLUES IN "D" MINOR

Use "D" natural minor scale - 8th position

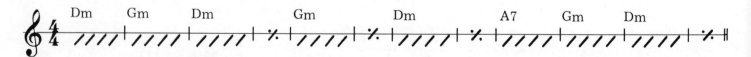

*Remember to stress the Flatted 5th against the VI7

Now that you can improvise to any key, we will learn the scales in different positions on the fingerboard. This will give you added freedom and increase originality by combining different positions.

BLUES SCALES - GROUP III (3)

Group III Blues scales have their root on the 3rd string.

GROUP III BLUES SCALES FORM

EXAMPLE ON "C"

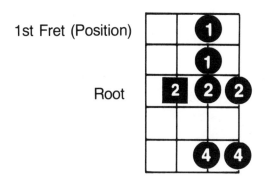

1st Fret (Position)

Root

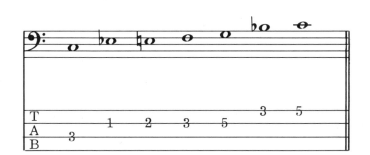

Position	1st	2nd	3rd	4th	5th	6th	7th	8th	9th	10th	11th	12th
Scale	C	C♯	D	E♭	E	F	F♯	G	A♭	A	B♭	B
Enharmonic Name		D♭					G♭					C♭

This form, played in the following positions, will create these Blues scales: Practice this Blues scale form chromatically up and down the fingerboard. One scale per measure.

● *RECORDED EXAMPLE #33*

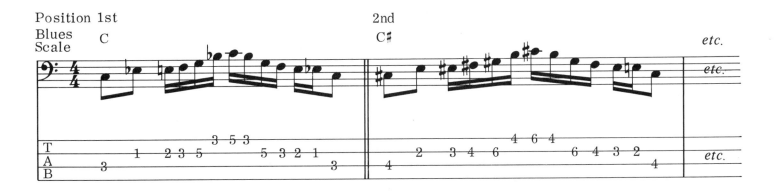

Now that you have mastered the basic scale form, we will add in the three variations which are related and also movable.

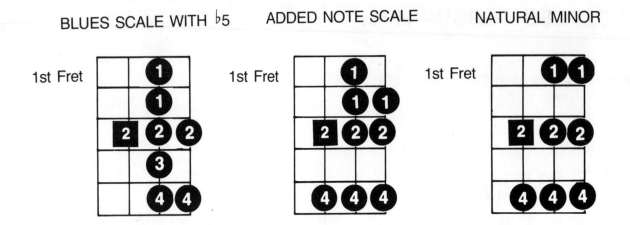

BLUES SCALE WITH ♭5   ADDED NOTE SCALE   NATURAL MINOR

1st Fret   1st Fret   1st Fret

You should now improvise to the pre-recorded progressions, using the Group III Blues scales.

● *RECORDED EXAMPLE #22*

BLUES IN "C" MAJOR

1. Use "C" Blues scale and variations - 1st position.
2. Combine "C" Blues scales - 1st and 6th positions.*

● *RECORDED EXAMPLE #23*

BLUES IN "F" MAJOR

1. Use "F" Blues scale and variations - 6th position
2. Combine "F" Blues scales - 6th and 11th positions.

● *RECORDED EXAMPLE #24*

BLUES IN "B♭" MAJOR

1. Use "B♭" Blues scale and variations - 11th position.
2. Combine "B" Blues scales - 11th and 4th positions.

● *RECORDED EXAMPLE #25*

BLUES IN "E♭" MINOR

1. Use "E♭" natural minor scale - 4th position
2. Combine "E♭" natural minor scales - 4th and 9th positions.

● *RECORDED EXAMPLE #26*

BLUES IN "A♭" MAJOR

1. Use "A♭" Blues scale and variations - 9th position.
2. Combine "A♭" Blues scales - 9th and 2nd positions.

*Combining Groups III and IV

● *RECORDED EXAMPLE #27*

BLUES IN "D♭" MAJOR

1. Use "D♭" Blues scale and variations - 2nd position.
2. Combine "D♭" Blues scales - 2nd and 7th positions.

● *RECORDED EXAMPLE #28*

BLUES IN "G♭" MAJOR

1. Use "G♭" Blues scale and variations - 7th position.
2. Combine "G♭" Blues scales - 7th and 12th positions.

● *RECORDED EXAMPLE #29*

BLUES IN "B" MINOR

1. Use "B" natural minor scale - 12th position.
2. Combine "B" natural minor scales - 12th and 5th positions.

● *RECORDED EXAMPLE #30*

BLUES IN "E" MAJOR

1. Use "E" Blues scale and variations - 5th position.
2. Combine "E" Blues scales - 5th and 10th positions.

● *RECORDED EXAMPLE #31*

BLUES IN "A" MAJOR

1. Use "A" Blues scale and variations - 10th position.
2. Combine "A" Blues scales - 10th and 3rd positions.

● *RECORDED EXAMPLE #32*

BLUES IN "D" MINOR

1. Use "D" natural minor scale - 3rd position.
2. Combine "D" natural minor scales - 3rd and 8th positions.

● *RECORDED EXAMPLE #13*

BLUES IN "G" MAJOR

1. Use "G" Blues scale - 8th position.
2. Combine "G" Blues scales - 8th and 1st positions.

BLUES SCALE - GROUP II (2)

Group II Blues scales have their root on the 2nd string.

GROUP II BLUES SCALE FORM	EXAMPLE ON "F"

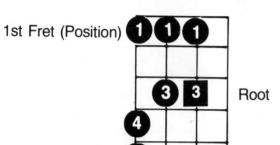

1st Fret (Position)

Root

Play these scales in
descending order first

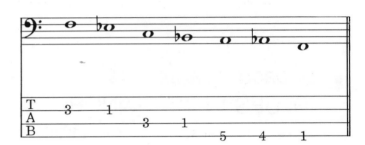

This form, played in the following positions, will create these blues scales:

Position	1st	2nd	3rd	4th	5th	6th	7th	8th	9th	10th	11th	12th
Scale	F	F♯	G	A♭	A	B♭	B	C	C♯	D	E♭	E
Enharmonic Name		G♭					C♭		D♭			

● *RECORDED EXAMPLE #34*

Practice this Blues scale form chromatically, up and down the fingerboard. One scale per measure.

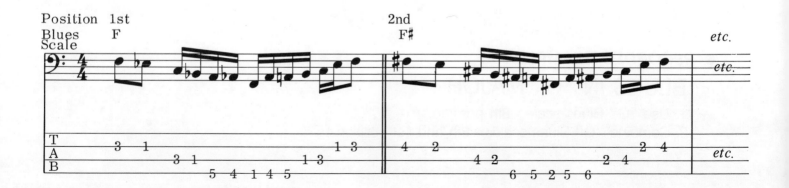

Now that you have mastered the basic scale form, we will add in the three variations which are related and movable.

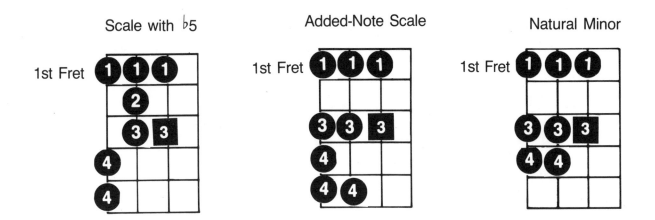

Scale with ♭5   Added-Note Scale   Natural Minor

You should now improvise to the recorded progressions using the Group II Blues scales.

● *RECORDED EXAMPLE #22*

BLUES IN "C" MAJOR

1. Use "C" Blues scale and variations - 8th position.
2. Combine "C" Blues scales - 8th, 1st and 6th positions.*

● *RECORDED EXAMPLE #23*

BLUES IN "F" MAJOR

1. Use "F" Blues scale and variations - 1st position.
2. Combine "F" Blues scales - 1st, 6th and 11th positions.

● *RECORDED EXAMPLE #24*

BLUES IN "B♭" MAJOR

1. Use "B♭" Blues scale and variations - 6th position.
2. Combine "B♭" Blues scales - 6th, 11th and 4th positions.

● *RECORDED EXAMPLE #25*

BLUES IN "E♭" MINOR

1. Use "E♭" natural minor scale - 11th position.
2. Combine "E♭" natural minor scales - 11th, 4th and 9th positions.

*Combine Groups II-III-IV

● *RECORDED EXAMPLE #26*

BLUES IN "A♭" MAJOR

1. Use "A♭" Blues scale and variations - 4th position.
2. Combine "A♭" Blues scales - 4th, 9th and 2nd positions.

● *RECORDED EXAMPLE #27*

BLUES IN "D♭" MAJOR

1. Use "D♭" Blues scale and variations - 9th position.
2. Combine "D♭" Blues scales - 9th, 2nd and 7th positions.

● *RECORDED EXAMPLE #28*

BLUES IN "G♭" MAJOR

1. Use "G♭" Blues scale and variations - 2nd position.
2. Combine "G♭" Blues scales - 2nd, 7th and 12th positions.

● *RECORDED EXAMPLE #29*

BLUES IN "B" MINOR

1. Use "B" natural minor - 7th position.
2. Combine "B" natural minor scales - 7th, 12th and 5th positions.

● *RECORDED EXAMPLE #30*

BLUES IN "E" MAJOR

1. Use "E" Blues scale and variations - 12th position.
2. Combine "E" Blues scales - 12th, 5th and 10th positions.

● *RECORDED EXAMPLE #31*

BLUES IN "A" MAJOR

1. Use "A" Blues scale and variations - 5th position.
2. Combine "A" Blues scales - 5th, 10th and 3rd positions.

● *RECORDED EXAMPLE #32*

BLUES IN "D" MINOR

1. Use "D" natural minor scale - 10th position.
2. Combine "D" natural minor scales - 10th, 3rd and 8th positions.

● *RECORDED EXAMPLE #13*

BLUES IN "G" MAJOR

1. Use "G" Blues scale and variations - 3rd position.
2. Combine "G" Blues scales - 3rd, 8th and 1st positions.

BLUES SCALES - GROUP I (1)

Group I Blues scales have their root on the the 1st string.

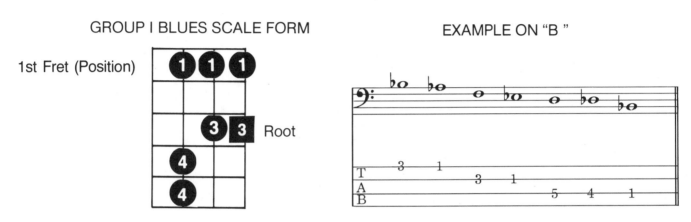

GROUP I BLUES SCALE FORM

1st Fret (Position)

Root

Play these scales in descending order first.

EXAMPLE ON "B"

This form, played in the following positions, will create these Blues scales:

Position	1st	2nd	3rd	4th	5th	6th	7th	8th	9th	10th	11th	12th
Scale	B♭	B	C	C♯	D	E♭	E	F	F♯	G	A♭	A
Enharmonic Name		C♭		D♭					G♭			

Practice this Blues scale form chromatically up and down the fingerboard. One scale per measure.

● *RECORDED EXAMPLE #35*

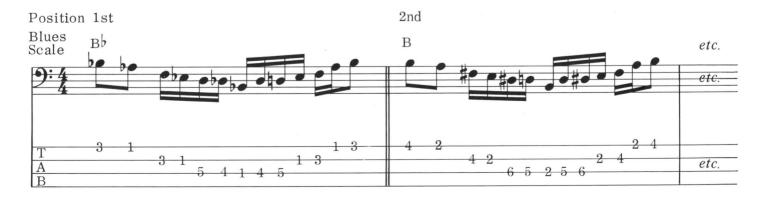

Now that you have the basic scale form, we'll add in three variations which are related and movable.

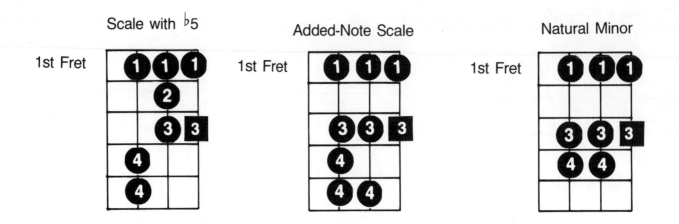

You should now improvise to the recorded progressions using the Group I Blues scale.

● *RECORDED EXAMPLE #22*
BLUES IN "C" MAJOR

1. Use "C" Blues scale and variations - 3rd position.
2. Combine "C" Blues scales - 3rd, 8th, 1st and 6th positions.*

● *RECORDED EXAMPLE #23*
BLUES IN "F" MAJOR

1. Use "F" Blues scale and variations - 8th position.
2. Combine "F" Blues scales - 8th, 1st, 6th and 11th positions.

● *RECORDED EXAMPLE #24*
BLUES IN "B♭" MAJOR

1. Use "B♭" Blues scale and variations - 1st and 13th positions.
2. Combine "B♭" Blues scales - 1st, 13th, 6th, 11th and 4th positions.

● *RECORDED EXAMPLE #25*
BLUES IN "E♭" MINOR

1. Use "E♭" natural minor scale - 6th position.
2. Combine "E♭" natural minor scales - 6th, 11th, 4th and 9th positions.

● *RECORDED EXAMPLE #26*
BLUES IN "A♭" MAJOR

1. Use "A♭" Blues scale and variations - 11th position.
2. Combine "A♭" Blues scales - 11th, 4th, 9th and 2nd positions.

*Combine Groups I, II, III, and IV

● *RECORDED EXAMPLE #27*

BLUES IN "D♭" MAJOR

1. Use "D♭" Blues scale and variations - 4th position.
2. Combine "D♭" Blues scales - 4th, 9th, 2nd and 7th positions.

● *RECORDED EXAMPLE #28*

BLUES IN "G♭" MAJOR

1. Use "G♭" Blues scale and variations - 9th position.
2. Combine "G♭" Blues scales - 9th, 2nd, 7th and 12th positions.

● *RECORDED EXAMPLE #29*

BLUES IN "B" MINOR

1. Use "B" natural minor - 2nd position.
2. Combine "B" natural minor scales - 2nd, 7th, 12th and 5th positions.

● *RECORDED EXAMPLE #30*

BLUES IN "E" MAJOR

1. Use "E" Blues scale and variations - 7th position.
2. Combine "E" Blues scales - 7th, 12th, 5th and 10th positions.

● *RECORDED EXAMPLE #31*

BLUES IN "A" MAJOR

1. Use "A" Blues scale and variations - 12th position.
2. Combine "A" Blues scales - 12th, 5th, 10th and 3rd positions.

● *RECORDED EXAMPLE #32*

BLUES IN "D" MINOR

1. Use "D" natural minor scale - 5th position.
2. Combine "D" natural minor scales - 5th, 10th, 3rd and 8th positions.

● *RECORDED EXAMPLE #13*

BLUES IN "G" MAJOR

1. Use "G" Blues scale and variations - 10th position.
2. Combine "G" Blues scales - 10th, 3rd, 8th and 1st positions.

BLUES SCALES - MINOR PENTATONIC* - EXTENDED RANGE

The following Blues scales have been extended over the entire range of the bass. Memorize and use them to connect the four (4) scale groups, or by themselves, when improvising.

#1 "G" BLUES SCALE - EXTENDED

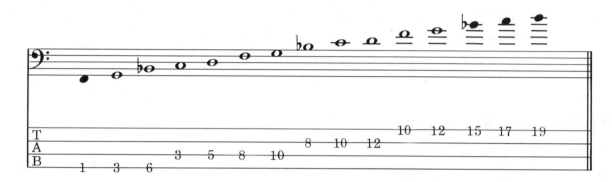

Quarter Notes = blues scale extended to lowest and highest range of the bass.

Improvise blues solos to Recorded Progression #13 using:

1. "G" blues scale extended
2. "G" blues scales and variations - 10th, 3rd, 8th, and 1st positions combined with the extended scale.

#2 "C" BLUES SCALE - EXTENDED

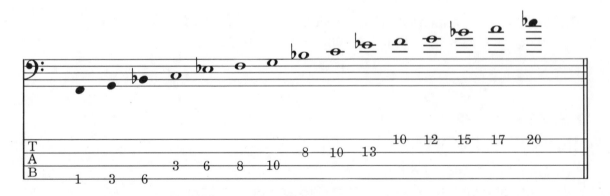

Improvise Blues solos to Recorded Progression #22 using:

1. "C" Blues scale extended.
2. "C" Blues scale and variations - 3rd, 8th, 1st and 6th positions combined with the extended scale.

Minor Pentatonic - the most basic of the Blues scales - 1st, Minor 3rd - 4th - 5th - Minor 7th. It may be used with any progression - Major or MInor. Used extensively in Rock and Country Rock improvising.

#3 "F" BLUES SCALE - EXTENDED

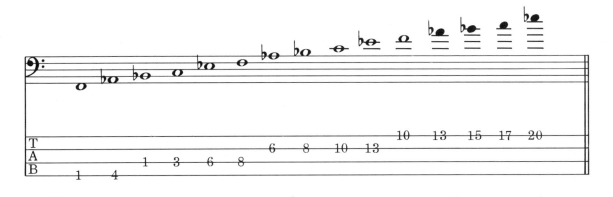

Improvise Blues solos to Recorded Progression #23 using:

1. "F" Blues scale extended.
2. "F" Blues scale and variations - 8th, 1st, 6th and 11th positions combined
   with the extended scale.

#4 "B♭" BLUES SCALE - EXTENDED

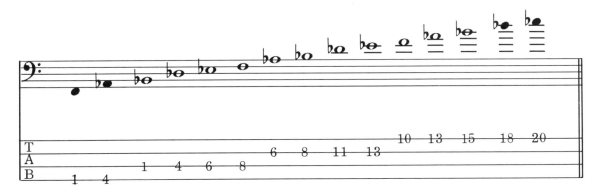

Improvise Blues solos to Recorded Progression #24 using:

1. "B♭" Blues scale extended.
2. "B♭" Blues scale and variations - 1st, 13th, 6th, 11th and 4th positions combined
   with the extended scale.

#5 "E♭" BLUES SCALE - EXTENDED

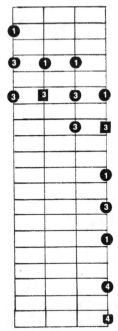

Improvise Blues solos to Recorded Progression #25 using:

1. "E♭" Blues scale extended.
2. "E♭" natural minor scales - 6th, 11th, 4th and 9th positions combined
   with the extended scale.

#6 "A♭" BLUES SCALE - EXTENDED

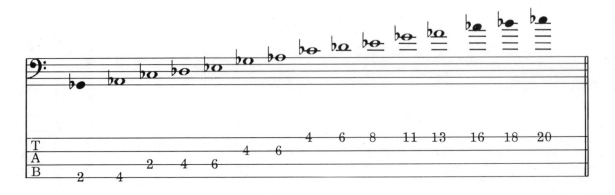

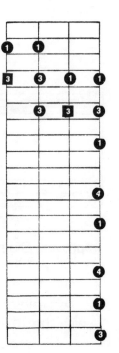

Improvise Blues solos to Recorded Progression #26 using:

1. "A♭" Blues scale extended.
2. "A♭" Blues scale and variations - 11th, 4th, 9th and 2nd positions combined
   with the extended scale.

#7 "D♭" BLUES SCALE - EXTENDED

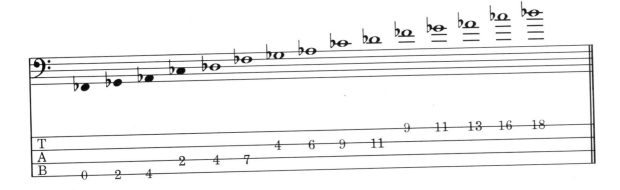

Improvise Blues solos to Recorded Progression #27 using:

1. "D♭" Blues scale extended.
2. "D♭" Blues scale and variations - 4th, 9th, 2nd and 7th positions combined with the extended scale.

#8 "G♭" BLUES SCALE - EXTENDED

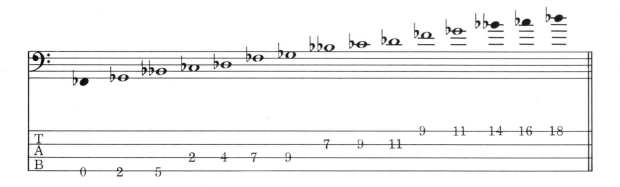

Improvise Blues solos to Recorded Progression #28 using:

1. "G♭" Blues scale extended.
2. "G♭" Blues scale and variations - 9th, 2nd, 7th and 12th positions combined with the extended scale.

#9 "B" BLUES SCALE - EXTENDED

Improvise Blues solos to Recorded Progression #29 using:

1. "B" Blues scale extended.
2. "B" natural minor scales - 2nd, 7th, 12th and 5th positions combined
   with the extended scale.

#10 "E" BLUES SCALE - EXTENDED

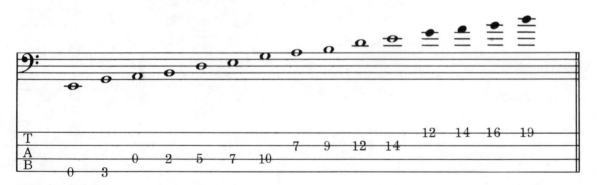

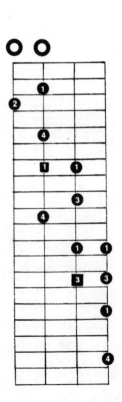

Improvise Blues solos to Recorded Progression #30 using:

1. "E" Blues scale extended.
2. "E" Blues scale and variations - 7th, 12th, 5th and 10th positions combined
   with the extended scale.

#11 "A" BLUES SCALE - EXTENDED

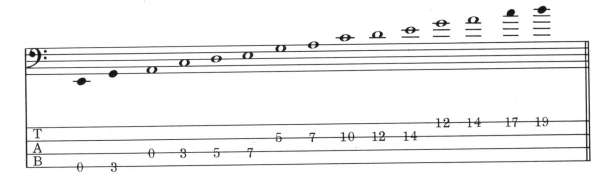

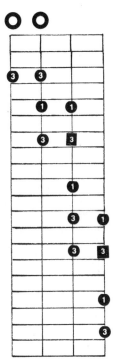

Improvise Blues solos to Recorded Progression #31 using:

1. "A" Blues scale extended.
2. "A" Blues scale and variations - 12th, 10th, 5th and 3rd positions combined with the extended scale.

#12 "D" BLUES SCALE - EXTENDED

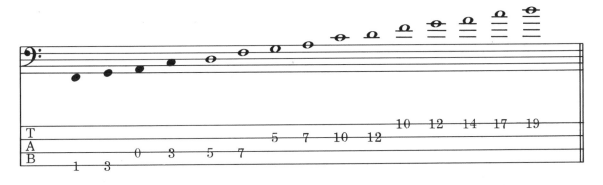

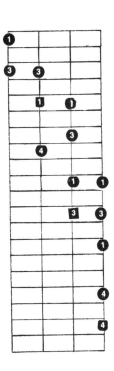

Improvise Blues solos to Recorded Progression #32 using:

1. "D" Blues scale extended.
2. "D" natural minor scales - 5th, 10th, 3rd and 8th positions combined with the extended scale.

SCALE SUBSTITUTION

In the Blues style it is very common for a phrase to be repeated with a different chord background. This creates a different effect or tonal color. Any note, phrase or scale will change their tonal color as different chords are sounded.

● *RECORDED EXAMPLE #3*

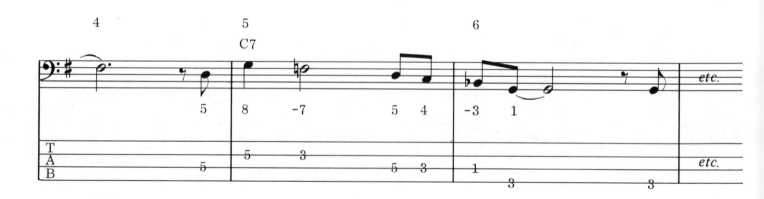

Listen to the first measure as compared to the fifth measure. The notes are the same, but with different chords. Notice how the overall sound changes. This technique is extended to cover not only phrases, but whole scales. In search of new, interesting, fresh sounds and ideas, many Blues artists constantly experiment playing different Blues scales against a given progression for tonal variety. The possibilities are limitless, but the following are the most commonly used:

•RECORDED EXAMPLE #13 - "G" BLUES

Improvise to this progression, substituting the following scales for the original "G" Blues scale:

1. "D" Blues scale - based on the 5th note of the original scale.
2. "C" Blues scale - based on the 4th note of the original scale.
3. "E" Blues scale - based on the 6th note of the original scale.
4. "A" Blues scale - based on the 2nd note of the original scale.

When superimposing a scale over a chord progression, your ear is the final judge of what sounds you want to convey to the listener. The "Blues" is a constant, never-ending search for the perfect solo.

MAJOR SCALES

The major scales are the basic building blocks of music. These are the tools you will use in creating your own bass lines and solos (Section II). The major scales are built on a specific number of half and whole steps.

Half-Step (½)-Notes directly next to each other (1-fret apart)

Whole-Step (1)-A whole step is two consecutive half or semi-tones (2 frets apart)

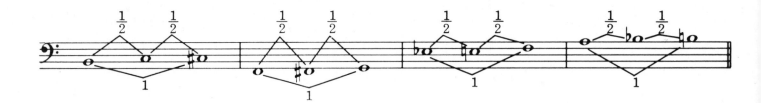

The major scales are composed of the specific order of whole-whole-half-whole-whole-whole-half-steps.
(1-1-½-1-1-1-½) = This is called The Diatonic Scale.

Example

C major

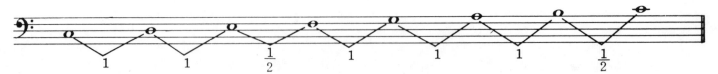

G major

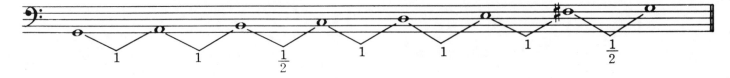

F major

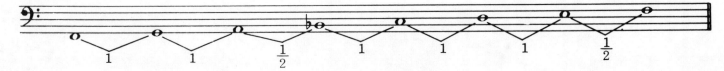

INTERVALS

This distance between two notes is called an "Interval". This distance is calculated by the number of diatonic scale tones between the two notes.

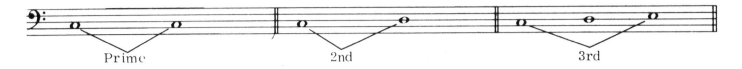

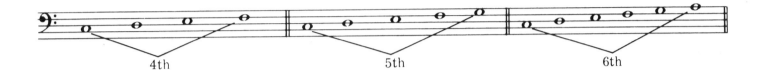

The intervals are also given names to determine the number of half-steps (page 36) contained between them EXAMPLES: Major 2nd = 1 whole step-Major 3rd = 5 half-steps-Major 6th = 10 half-steps - Major 7th = 12 half-steps. Listed below are the more frequently used methods of determining these names:

Major - When referring to a 2nd, 3rd, 6th, or 7th interval, the term Major is used when the higher of the two tones is in the Major Scale of the lower note.

(Ex.)

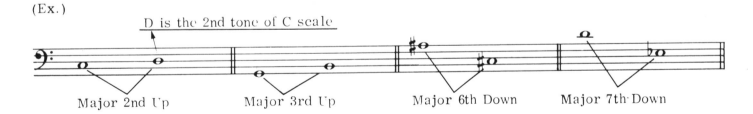

Minor - When the upper note is one-half step below Major, it is called Minor.

(Ex.)

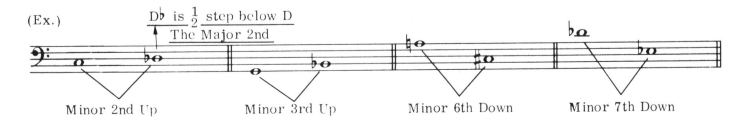

Perfect - If the higher tone is in the scale of the lower, the interval of the 4th, 5th or octave is called Perfect.

(Ex.)

Eb is the 4th tone in the Bb scale

Perfect 4th Up   Perfect 5th Up   Perfect 4th Down   Perfect 5th Down

Diminished-One half-step below Perfect or Minor is diminished.

(Ex.)

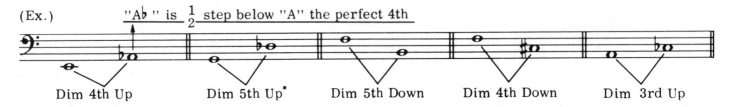

"Ab " is ½ step below "A" the perfect 4th

Dim 4th Up   Dim 5th Up*   Dim 5th Down   Dim 4th Down   Dim 3rd Up

Augumented-One half-step above Major or Perfect.

(Ex.)

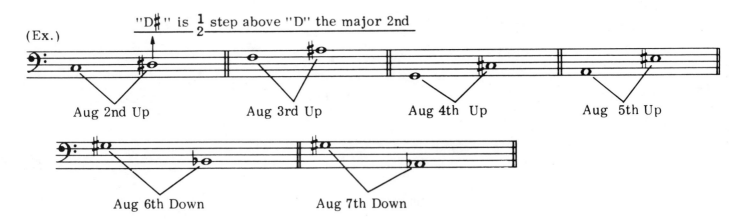

"D#" is ½ step above "D" the major 2nd

Aug 2nd Up   Aug 3rd Up   Aug 4th Up   Aug 5th Up

Aug 6th Down   Aug 7th Down

MINOR SCALES

For every Major scale there will be three relative Minor scales.

The relative Minor scales will start on the 6th tone of the Major scale. They will also keep the same signature.

C major

Same Key Signature-No Alterations

A minor(Natural)

(1)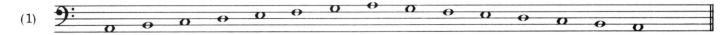

Same as the natural minor except raise the 7th note ½ step ascending and descending the scale.

A minor(Harmonic)

(2)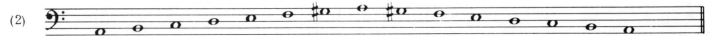

Same as the natural minor except raise the 6th and 7th notes ½ step ascending the scale and natural descending. All scales are discussed in detail in Section II.

A minor(Melodic)

(3)

*Tritone-The Dim. 5th-Aug. 4th is called the Tritone because it contains three whole-tones. Because of its dissonance, it should be treated carefully. In the Middle Ages, it was referred to as the "Devils Music" (Diabolus Musica).